Scriptures for All Occasions

Anne Van Wagner Young

LEISURE ARTS • Maumelle Arkansas

Table Of Contents

MOTHER (105w x 75h)

Aida 11 or Hardanger over 2	9⅝" x 6⅞"
Aida 14	7½" x 5⅜"
Aida 18	5⅞" x 4¼"
Hardanger 22	4⅞" x 3½"

MOTHER (105w x 75h)

ANCHOR	X	DMC	B'ST	COLOR
048	■	818		vy lt pink
049	⊙	3689		vy lt mauve
066	▫	3688		lt mauve
068	✱	3687		mauve
069		3685	⁄	dk mauve
0214	V	368		vy lt green
0876	□	503		lt blue green
0877	☆	502		blue green
0878	●	501	⁄	dk blue green
0830	x	644		vy lt khaki
0903	■	640	⁄	khaki

DAUGHTER (94w x 38h)	
Aida 11 or Hardanger over 2	8⅝″ x 3½″
Aida 14	6¾″ x 2¾″
Aida 18	5¼″ x 2⅛″
Hardanger 22	4⅜″ x 1¾″

ANNIVERSARY (50w x 80h)	
Aida 11 or Hardanger over 2	4⅝″ x 7⅜″
Aida 14	3⅝″ x 5¾″
Aida 18	2⅞″ x 4½″
Hardanger 22	2⅜″ x 3¾″

DAUGHTER (94w x 38h)

ANCHOR	X	DMC	B'ST	COLOR
0890	8	729		gold
066	◊	3688		lt mauve
068	x	3687		mauve
069	*	3685	/	dk mauve
0860	■	3052		dk olive
0861	◆	3051	/	vy dk olive

ANNIVERSARY (50w x 80h)

ANCHOR	X	DMC	B'ST	COLOR
02	⁚	blanc		white
0306	■	725		yellow
0307	C	783		vy dk yellow
0891	■	676		lt gold
0890	8	729		gold
0968	■	778		lt dusty mauve
0969	⊙	316		dusty mauve
0970	▲	315		dk dusty mauve
0849	■	927		lt grey blue
0850	V	926		grey blue
0860	■	3052		dk olive
0861	◆	3051		vy dk olive
0403	■	310	/	black

...Personalize using black, Alphabet #3 and numbers from Alphabet #2, pg 20.

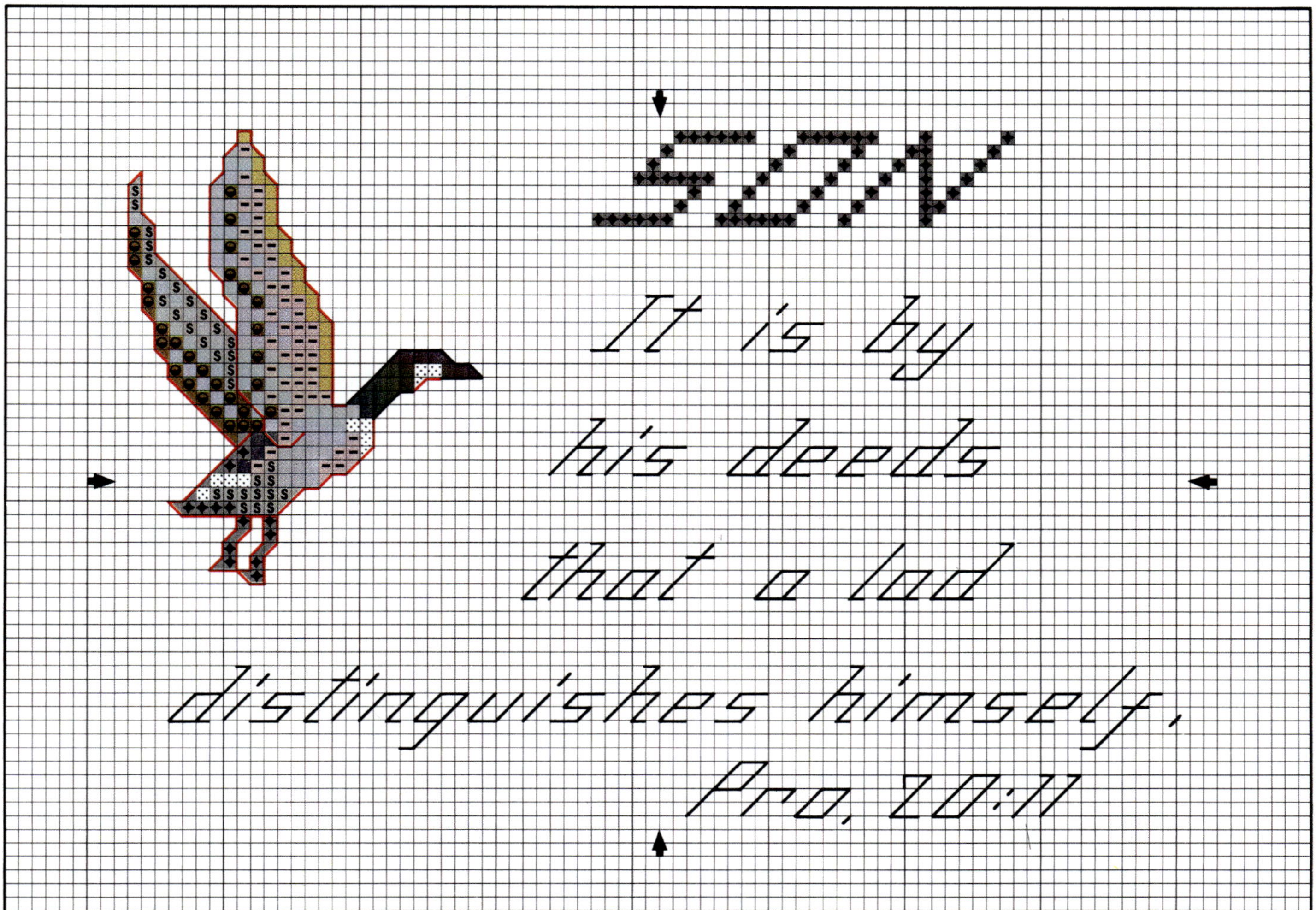

SON (78w x 51h)	
Aida 11 or	
Hardanger over 2	7⅛" x 4¾"
Aida 14	5⅝" x 3¾"
Aida 18	4⅜" x 2⅞"
Hardanger 22	3⅝" x 2⅜"

ORDINATION/SERVICE (54w x 54h)	
Aida 11 or	
Hardanger over 2	5" x 5"
Aida 14	3⅞" x 3⅞"
Aida 18	3" x 3"
Hardanger 22	2½" x 2½"

SON (78w x 51h)

ANCHOR	X	DMC	¼X	B'ST	COLOR
02		blanc			white
0392		642			lt khaki
0393		640			khaki
0397		3072			ultra lt grey
0900		647			lt grey
8581	S	646			grey
0400		645		/	dk grey
0403		310		/	black

ORDINATION/SERVICE (54w x 54h)

ANCHOR	X	DMC	B'ST	COLOR
0850	V	926		grey blue
0851		924	/	dk grey blue

GOING AWAY (51w x 45h)

Aida 11 or Hardanger over 2	4¾″ x 4⅛″
Aida 14	3¾″ x 3¼″
Aida 18	2⅞″ x 2½″
Hardanger 22	2⅜″ x 2⅛″

HOUSEWARMING (49w x 78h)

Aida 11 or Hardanger over 2	4½″ x 7⅛″
Aida 14	3½″ x 5⅝″
Aida 18	2¾″ x 4⅜″
Hardanger 22	2¼″ x 3⅝″

GOING AWAY (51w x 45h)

ANCHOR	X	DMC	B'ST	COLOR
02	⁙	blanc		white
0303	6	972		orange
0108	■	211		lt lavender
0105	H	209		lavender
098	■	553		violet
0101	▪	550	/	vy dk violet
0242	8	989		lt green
0244	◆	987	/	dk green

HOUSEWARMING (49w x 78h)

ANCHOR	X	DMC	B'ST	COLOR
0896	■	221	/	dk dusty rose
0861	■	3051		vy dk olive
0850	C	926		grey blue
0832	■	612		dk khaki
0382	■	3371	/	black brown

···Centering words, personalize using dk dusty rose and Alphabet #2, pg. 20.

BIRTH (95w x 81h)

ANCHOR	X	DMC	¼X	B'ST	COLOR
0386		746			off-white
0292		677			vy lt gold
0891	Δ	676			lt gold
0890	V	729			gold
0901		680			dk gold
023		818			vy lt pink
024	⊙	776			lt pink
027		899			pink
0875		503			lt blue green
0876	*	502			blue green
0158	◊	747			lt turquoise
0167		598			turquoise
0168		597			dk turquoise
0891	•	676	lt gold French Knot		

...Personalize using blue green and Alphabet #4, pg. 20.

BIRTH (95w 81h)	
Aida 11 or	
Hardanger over 2	8¾" x 7⅜"
Aida 14	6⅞" x 5⅞"
Aida 18	5⅜" x 4½"
Hardanger 22	4⅜" x 3¾"

TEACHER (76w x 48h)	
Aida 11 or Hardanger over 2	7″ x 4⅜″
Aida 14	5½″ x 3½″
Aida 18	4¼″ x 2¾″
Hardanger 22	3½″ x 2¼″

TEACHER (76w x 48h)

ANCHOR	X	DMC	¼X	B'ST	COLOR
0387	O	712	■		cream
0890	■	729			gold
0901	*	680		/	dk gold
047	■	498			red
044	★	815	■		dk red
0920	■	932			lt antique blue
0921	B	931			antique blue
0922	▲	930	■		dk antique blue
0242	⊙	989			lt avocado
0215	◊	320	■		lt green
0217	S	367	■		green
0218	◆	319	■		dk green
0403		310		/	black

FRIENDSHIP #1 (60w x 47h)

ANCHOR	X	DMC	B'ST	COLOR
0890	■	729		gold
0860	■	3052		dk olive
0861	◆	3051	/	vy dk olive
097	■	554		lt violet
098	H	553		violet
0100	■	552		dk violet
0101		550	/	vy dk violet

FRIENDSHIP #1 (60w x 47h)	
Aida 11 or Hardanger over 2	5½″ x 4⅜″
Aida 14	4⅜″ x 3⅜″
Aida 18	3⅜″ x 2⅝″
Hardanger 22	2¾″ x 2¼″

RETIREMENT (79w x 60h)

Aida 11 or Hardanger over 2	7¼″ x 5½″
Aida 14	5¾″ x 4⅜″
Aida 18	4½″ x 3⅜″
Hardanger 22	3⅝″ x 2¾″

FIRST COMMUNION (57w x 49h)

Aida 11 or Hardanger over 2	5¼″ x 4½″
Aida 14	4⅛″ x 3½″
Aida 18	3⅛″ x 2¾″
Hardanger 22	2⅝″ x 2¼″

RETIREMENT (79w x 60h)

ANCHOR	X	DMC	B'ST	COLOR
0253	☆	472		ultra lt green
0254		471		vy lt green
0266	6	470		lt green
0267	V	469		green
0268		937		dk green
0263		936	⁄	vy dk green
0269	●	935		ultra dk green
0371		433		vy dk brown
0359	■	801	⁄	ultra dk brown

...Personalize using ultra dk brown, Alphabet #3 and numbers from Alphabet #2, pg. 20.

FIRST COMMUNION (57w x 49h)

ANCHOR	X	DMC	B'ST	COLOR
0849	+	927		lt grey blue
0850		926		grey blue
0851		924	⁄	dk grey blue
0242		989		lt green
0861	♦	3051	⁄	vy dk olive

...Personalize using dk grey blue and Alphabet #1, pg. 20.

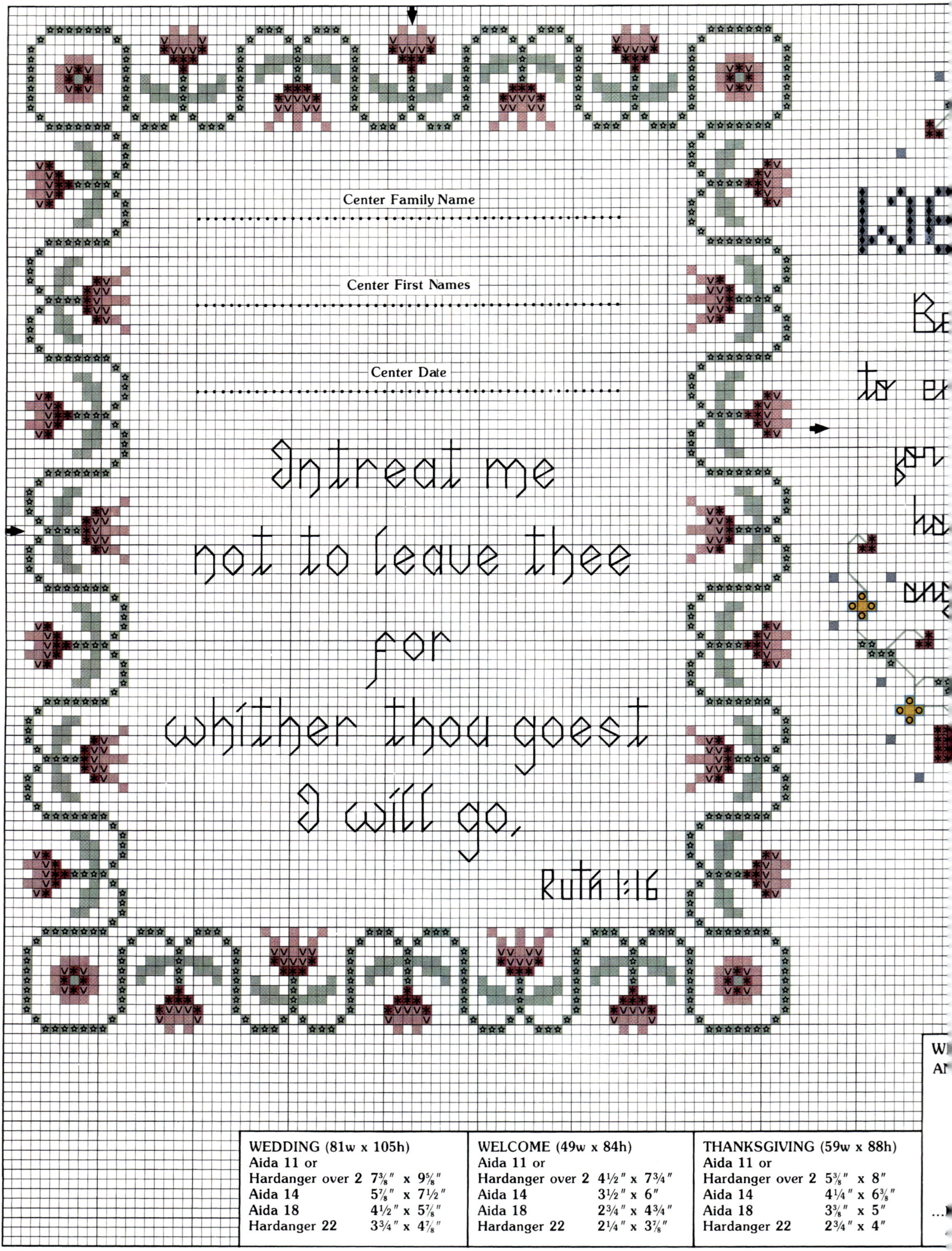

WEDDING (81w x 105h)		WELCOME (49w x 84h)		THANKSGIVING (59w x 88h)	
Aida 11 or		Aida 11 or		Aida 11 or	
Hardanger over 2	7⅜″ x 9⅝″	Hardanger over 2	4½″ x 7¾″	Hardanger over 2	5⅜″ x 8″
Aida 14	5⅞″ x 7½″	Aida 14	3½″ x 6″	Aida 14	4¼″ x 6⅜″
Aida 18	4½″ x 5⅞″	Aida 18	2¾″ x 4¾″	Aida 18	3⅜″ x 5″
Hardanger 22	3¾″ x 4⅞″	Hardanger 22	2¼″ x 3⅞″	Hardanger 22	2¾″ x 4″

G (81w x 105h)

X	DMC	B'ST	COLOR
	224		lt dusty rose
V	223		dusty rose
*	221		dk dusty rose
	503		lt blue green
☆	502		blue green
	501	/	dk blue green

...ize using dk blue green and ... #4, pg. 20.

WELCOME (49w x 84h)

ANCHOR	X	DMC	B'ST	COLOR
0292	O	677		vy lt gold
0890		729	/	gold
0896	*	221		dk dusty rose
0920		932		lt antique blue
0922	♦	930	/	dk antique blue
0877	☆	502	/	blue green

THANKSGIVING (59w x 88h)

ANCHOR	X	DMC	B'ST	COLOR
0890		729		gold
0901	⊙	680		dk gold
010		351		coral
013	S	349		dk coral
047	X	817		lt red
0217		367	/	green
0218		319	/	dk green
0218	•	319		dk green French Knot

...Personalize using dk green and Alphabet #1, and numbers from Alphabet #4, pg. 20.

GRANDPARENTS (54w x 82h)

ANCHOR	X	DMC	¼X	B'ST	COLOR
0874	■	676			lt gold
0159	■	827	◪		lt blue
0161	■	813	◪		blue
0162	■	826			dk blue
0267	■	3347	◪		vy lt green
0268	■	3346	◪		green
0246		986		⧄	vy dk green
0403		310		⧄	black

GRANDPARENTS (54w x 82h)

Aida 11 or			
Hardanger over 2	5″	x	7½″
Aida 14	3⅞″	x	5⅞″
Aida 18	3″	x	4⅝″
Hardanger 22	2½″	x	3¾″

FRIENDSHIP #2 (55w x 43h)

ANCHOR	X	DMC	B'ST	COLOR
0903	■	3022		lt brown grey
0905		3021	⧄	brown grey

FRIENDSHIP #2 (55w x 43h)

Aida 11 or			
Hardanger over 2	5″	x	4″
Aida 14	4″	x	3⅛″
Aida 18	3⅛″	x	2½″
Hardanger 22	2½″	x	2″

DEDICATION/CHRISTENING (87w x 119h)

Aida 11 or			
Hardanger over 2	8″	x	10⅞″
Aida 14	6¼″	x	8½″
Aida 18	4⅞″	x	6⅝″
Hardanger 22	4″	x	5½″

DEDICATION/CHRISTENING (87w x 119h)

ANCHOR	X	DMC	B'ST	COLOR
0969	■	316		mauve
0972	■	315		dk mauve
0860	■	3052	⧄	dk olive
0849	■	927		lt grey blue
0850	■	926		grey blue
0851		924	⧄	dk grey blue

...Personalize using dk grey blue and Alphabet #4, pg. 20.

For this child
I prayed;
Center Name
and the Lord hath
given me my petition
which I asked of Him;
So
I have dedicated him
to the Lord
as long as he liveth.
I Sam. 1:27,28

SISTER (66w x 61h)			
Aida 11 or			
Hardanger over 2	6″	x	5⅝″
Aida 14	4¾″	x	4⅜″
Aida 18	3¾″	x	3½″
Hardanger 22	3″	x	2⅞″

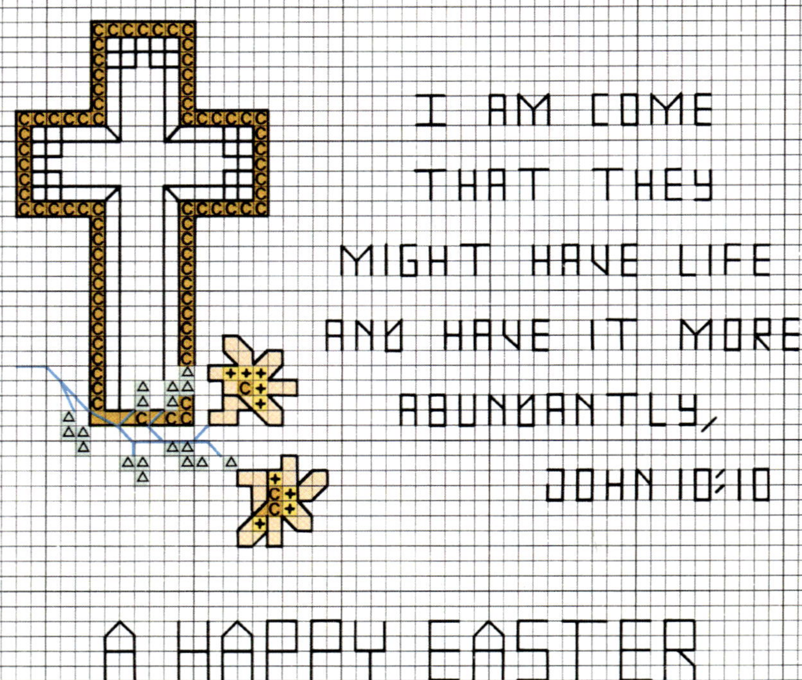

EASTER (53w x 44h)			
Aida 11 or			
Hardanger over 2	4⅞″	x	4″
Aida 14	3⅞″	x	3¼″
Aida 18	3″	x	2½″
Hardanger 22	2½″	x	2″

SISTER (66w x 61h)

ANCHOR	X	DMC	B'ST	COLOR
02		blanc		white
0293		727		dk yellow
0891	6	676		lt gold
0890	C	729		gold
0843		3013		vy lt olive
0845		3012	/	lt olive
0900		648	/	vy lt grey

EASTER (53w x 44h)

ANCHOR	X	DMC	¼X	B'ST	COLOR
0386		746	◺		off-white
0292	+	677			vy lt gold
0890	C	729	◺		gold
0876	△	503			lt blue green
0877		502		/	blue green
0905		3021		/	brown grey

BAPTISM (73w x 53h)

ANCHOR	X	DMC	B'ST	COLOR
027		899		pink
041	*	335		dk pink
047		304	/	red
0849		927		lt grey blue
0850	◘	926		grey blue
0851		924	/	dk grey blue
0858	◊	524		lt grey green
0860	S	522		grey green

BAPTISM (73w x 53h)

Aida 11 or Hardanger over 2	6¾" x 4⅞"
Aida 14	5¼" x 3⅞"
Aida 18	4⅛" x 3"
Hardanger 22	3⅜" x 2½"

BROTHER (54w x 54h)

Aida 11 or Hardanger over 2	5" x 5"
Aida 14	3⅞" x 3⅞"
Aida 18	3" x 3"
Hardanger 22	2½" x 2½"

BROTHER (54w x 54h)

ANCHOR	X	DMC	¼X	B'ST	COLOR
0903	x	3022	◢		lt brown grey
0905		3021		/	brown grey

GET WELL/SYMPATHY
(52w x 39h)

Fabric	Size
Aida 11 or Hardanger over 2	4¾" x 3⅝"
Aida 14	3¾" x 2⅞"
Aida 18	3" x 2¼"
Hardanger 22	2⅜" x 1⅞"

CHRISTMAS (53w x 85h)

Fabric	Size
Aida 11 or Hardanger over 2	4⅞" x 7¾"
Aida 14	3⅞" x 6⅛"
Aida 18	3" x 4¾"
Hardanger 22	2½" x 3⅞"

GRADUATION (89w x 118h)

Fabric	Size
Aida 11 or Hardanger over 2	8⅛" x 10¾"
Aida 14	6½" x 8½"
Aida 18	5" x 6⅝"
Hardanger 22	4⅛" x 5⅜"

GET WELL/SYMPATHY (52w x 39h)

ANCHOR	X	DMC	B'ST	COLOR
068		3687		mauve
0972		315		dk dusty mauve
0859		3053		olive
0861		3051	/	vy dk olive

CHRISTMAS (53w x 85h)

ANCHOR	X	DMC	¼X	B'ST	COLOR
0386		746			off-white
0292		3078			lt yellow
0874		676		/ (red)	lt gold
0890		729			gold
0901		680			dk gold
0778		948			flesh
0847		928			vy lt grey blue
0849		927			lt grey blue
0361		738			ultra lt brown
0363		436			lt brown
0365		435			brown
0310		434			dk brown
0403		310		/	black

GRADUATION (89w x 118h)

ANCHOR	X	DMC	¼X	B'ST	COLOR
0890		729			gold
0169		806		/ (red)	vy dk turquoise
0401		844			vy dk grey
0403		310		/	black

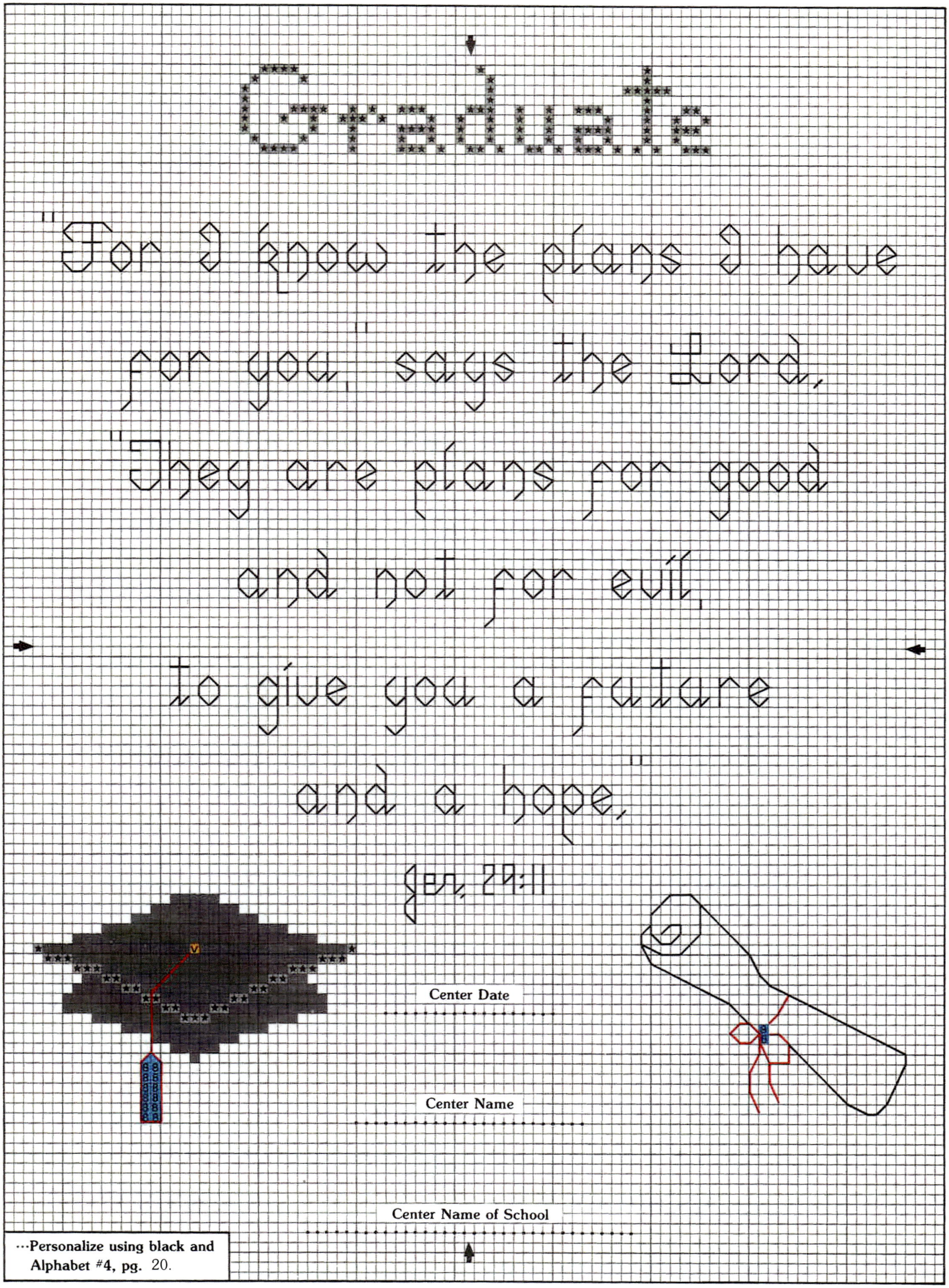

…Personalize using black and Alphabet #4, pg. 20.

FATHER (112w x 70h)

Fabric	Size
Aida 11 or Hardanger over 2	$10\frac{1}{4}$" x $6\frac{3}{8}$"
Aida 14	8" x 5"
Aida 18	$6\frac{1}{4}$" x 4"
Hardanger 22	$5\frac{1}{8}$" x $3\frac{1}{4}$"

FATHER (112w x 70h)

ANCHOR	X	DMC	¼X	B'ST	COLOR
0849	■	927	◩		lt grey blue
0921	▲	931		/	antique blue
0843	■	3013			vy lt olive
0859	☆	3053			olive
0830		644		/	vy lt khaki
0392	V	642			lt khaki
0889		610		/	vy dk khaki
0362	■	437	◩		vy lt brown
0363	S	436			lt brown
0365	X	435			brown

General Instructions

WORKING WITH CHARTS

How To Read Charts: Each of the designs is shown in chart form. Each colored square on the chart represents one Cross Stitch. Each square is shown in color, and in most cases, also with a symbol. The straight lines on the chart indicate Backstitch. These lines are shown either in color or black; the color to use is indicated on the color key.

Recommended Colors: We refer to all colors by name and also by Anchor stranded cotton and DMC embroidery floss numbers. Cover models were stitched using DMC. For each design, Anchor numbers were chosen to assure proper blending of colors in that design and not as perfect matches to DMC. For this reason, we do not recommend that both brands be used in the same design.

How To Determine Finished Sizes: While the number of stitches varies with each charted design, the finished size of your design depends on the **thread count per inch** of the fabric being used. To determine the finished size of the design on different fabrics, divide the number of squares (stitches) in the width of the charted design by the thread count of the fabric. For example: A charted design with a width of 80 squares worked on Aida 14 will yield a design 5¾" wide. Repeat for the number of squares (stitches) in the height of the charted design. (***Note:*** To work over two fabric threads, divide the number of squares by one-half the thread count.) Then add the amount of background you want plus a generous amount for finishing.

STITCH DIAGRAMS

Counted Cross Stitch: For horizontal rows, work each Cross Stitch in two journeys ***(Fig. 1)***. For vertical rows, complete each stitch as shown ***(Fig. 2)***. When working over two fabric threads, work Cross Stitch as shown in **Fig. 3**. When the chart shows a Backstitch crossing a colored square ***(Fig. 4)***, a Cross Stitch (**Fig. 1, 2 or 3**) should be worked first, then the Backstitch ***(Fig. 7)*** should be worked on top of the Cross Stitch.

Fig. 1

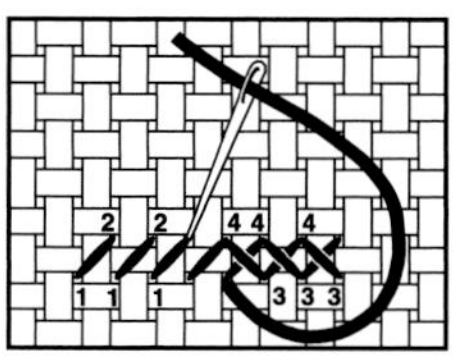

Fig. 2

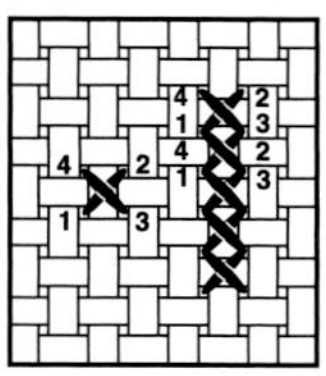

Fig.3

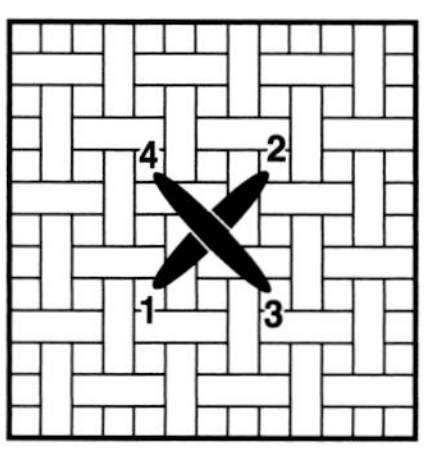

Fig.4

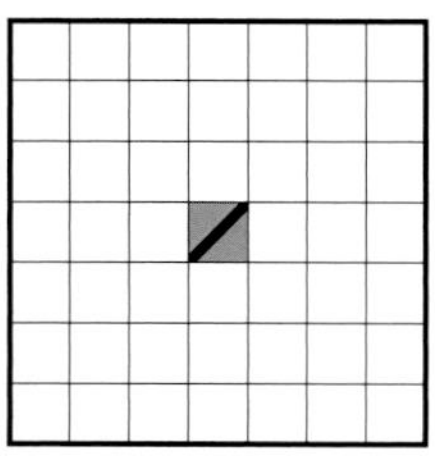

Quarter Stitch (¼X): Quarter Stitches are denoted by triangular shapes of color on the chart and on the color key. Come up at 1 ***(Fig. 5)***; then split fabric thread to go down at 2. **Fig. 6** shows the technique for Quarter Stitch when working over two fabric threads.

Fig. 5

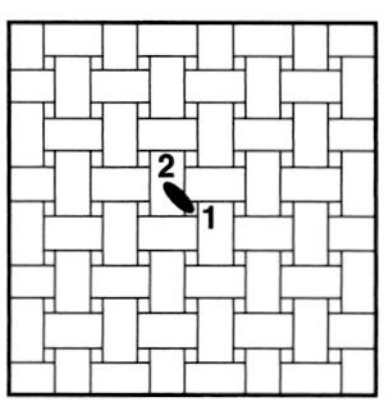

Fig. 6

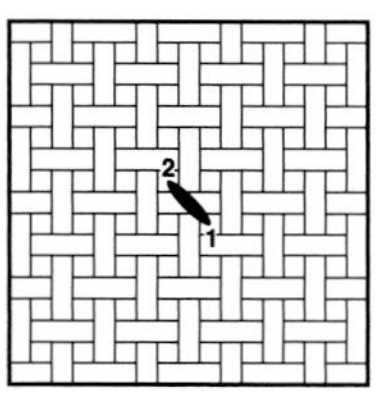

Backstitch: For outline detail, Backstitch (shown on chart and on color key by black or colored straight lines) should be worked after the design has been completed ***(Fig. 7)***.

Fig. 7

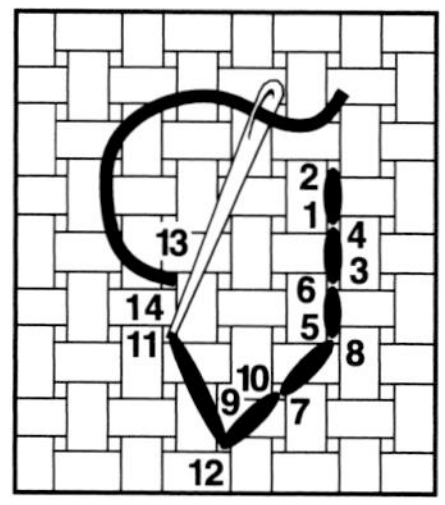

French Knot: Bring thread up at 1. Wrap once around needle and insert needle at 2, holding end of thread with non-stitching fingers ***(Fig. 8)***. Tighten knot, then pull needle through fabric holding thread until it must be released. For larger knot, use more strands; wrap only once.

Fig. 8

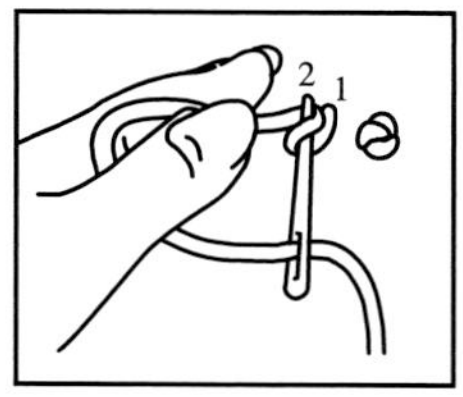

FINISHING TECHNIQUES

PILLOW FINISHING

Step 1. For pillow top, trim stitched piece to desired size plus ½" on all 4 sides for seam allowance. Cut pillow backing same size as pillow top.

Step 2. To make ruffle, cut a strip of fabric twice desired finished width plus 1" for seam allowances and twice outer dimension of pillow (measure pillow top on all 4 sides, then double measurement). (***Note:*** This strip may be pieced if necessary.) Tum short ends ½" to wrong side. Fold strip in half lengthwise with wrong sides together and press. Hand or machine-baste close to raw edge. Make another basting seam ¼" from the first. Pull basting threads, drawing up gathers to fit pillow top.

Step 3. See **Fig. 9** for placement of trims. Start at bottom edge of pillow top and 1" from end of trims. One at a time, baste trims to right side of pillow top with finished edges toward center of pillow and raw edges facing outward. Clip seam allowances at corners. Join ends of ruffle using blind stitches.

Fig. 9

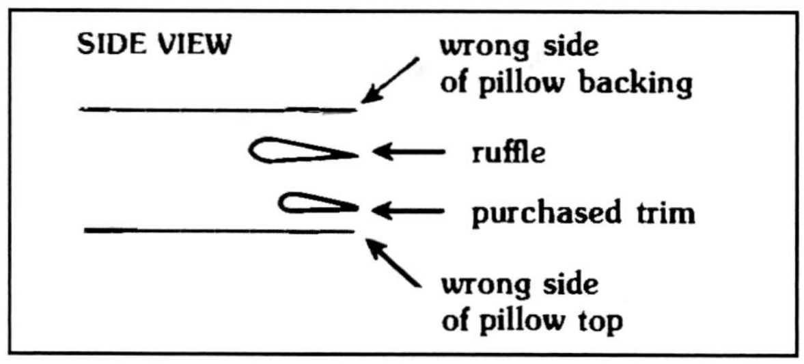

Step 4. With right sides together, machine-stitch pillow backing to pillow top, leaving an opening at bottom edge. Turn right side out, carefully pushing corners outward. Stuff with polyester fiberfill or insert pillow form and sew final closure by hand.

HOOP FINISHING

Cut stitched piece, batting and lining fabric 3" larger on all sides than hoop. Place batting between wrong sides of lining fabric and stitched piece. Insert in hoop, centering design and pulling materials taut; tighten screw. Cut excess materials close to hoop. Add trim as desired. To make ruffle, see **Pillow Finishing, Step 2.** Glue gathered edge of ruffle to back edge of hoop, overlapping ends of ruffle.

PROJECTS

Anniversary — Driftwood Dublin Linen —stitched over two fabric threads — approx design size 4" x 6½" - custom framed.
Baptism — Blush Aida 14 — approx design size 5¼" x $3^{7}/_{8}$" — inserted in 5" x 7" frame.
Birth - Cream Lugana — stitched over two fabric threads — approx design size 7¾" x 6½" — custom framed.
Brother - Clay Linda — stitched over two fabric threads — approx design size 4" x 4" — custom framed. **Also stitched** on Ivory Aida 14 — approx design size $3^{7}/_{8}$"x $3^{7}/_{8}$"— inserted in purchased box (5" x 5"opening).
Christmas — Ivory Aida 14 — approx design size $3^{7}/_{8}$" x $6^{1}/_{8}$" — inserted in 5" x 7" frame.
Daughter — Ivory Aida 14 — approx design size 6¾" x 2¾" — custom framed.
Dedication/Christening — Cream Lugana — stitched over two fabric threads — approx design size 7" x $9^{5}/_{8}$" — custom framed.
Easter - Ivory Aida 14 — approx design size $3^{7}/_{8}$" x 3¼" — custom framed.
Father — Driftwood Cork Linen — stitched over two fabric threads — approx design size $11^{1}/_{4}$" x 7" — custom framed.
First Communion — Ivory Aida 14 — approx design size $4^{1}/_{8}$" x 3½" — inserted in 5" x 5" frame.
Friendship #1 — Ivory Aida 14 — approx design size $4^{3}/_{8}$" x $3^{3}/_{8}$" — custom framed. **Also stitched** on Ivory Hardanger — stitched over two fabric threads — approx design size 5½" x $4^{3}/_{8}$" — see Pillow Finishing, pg. 19.
Friendship #2 — Platinum Aida 14 — approx design size 4" x $3^{1}/_{8}$" — inserted in 4" x 5" frame.
Get Well/Sympathy — Ivory Aida 14 — approx design size 3¾" x $2^{7}/_{8}$" —inserted in 4" x 5" frame.
Going Away — Ivory Aida 14 — approx design size 3¾" x 3¼" inserted in 5" wooden hoop — see Hoop Finishing.
Graduation — Ivory Aida 14 — approx design size 6½" x 8½" — inserted in 8" x 10" frame.
Grandparents — Ivory Aida 14 — approx design size $3^{7}/_{8}$" x $5^{7}/_{8}$" — custom framed.
Housewarming — Ivory Aida 14 — approx design size 3½" x $5^{5}/_{8}$" — inserted in purchased frame (4" x 6" oval opening). **Also stitched** on Mocha Dublin Linen — stitched over two fabric threads — approx design size 4" x 6¼" — custom framed.
Mother — Clay Linda — stitched over two fabric threads — approx design size 7¾" x $5^{5}/_{8}$" — custom framed. **Also stitched** on Ivory Hardanger — stitched over two fabric threads — approx design size $9^{5}/_{8}$" x $6^{7}/_{8}$" — custom framed.
Ordination/Service — Ivory Aida 14 — approx design size $3^{7}/_{8}$" x $3^{7}/_{8}$" — custom framed.
Retirement — Ivory Aida 14 — approx design size 5¾" x $4^{3}/_{8}$" — custom framed.
Sister — White Lugana — stitched over two fabric threads — approx design size $5^{3}/_{8}$" x $4^{7}/_{8}$" — custom framed. **Also stitched** on White Sundal — stitched over two fabric threads — approx design size 4¾" x $4^{3}/_{8}$" — for ribbon trim, weave $^{1}/_{16}$"w yellow satin ribbon into openwork stripes and add bows at corners before making pillow — see Pillow Finishing, pg. 19.
Son — Fiddler's Lite 14 — approx design size $5^{5}/_{8}$" x 3¾" — custom framed.
Teacher — Ivory Aida 14 — approx design size 5½" x 3½" — inserted in 5" x 7" frame.
Thanksgiving — Ivory Aida 14 — approx design size 4¼" x $6^{3}/_{8}$" — custom framed.
Wedding — White Dublin Linen — stitched over two fabric threads — approx design size 6½" x 8½" — custom framed.
Welcome — Ivory Aida 14 - approx design size 3½" x 6" — inserted in 5" x 7" oval frame.

Instructions tested and cover items made by Susan Alderson, Deborah Burns, Anita Drennan, Karen Henry, Denise Kornegay, Lynn Mizelle, Karen Sisco, Jane Walker and Patty Winkler.

ALPHABETS

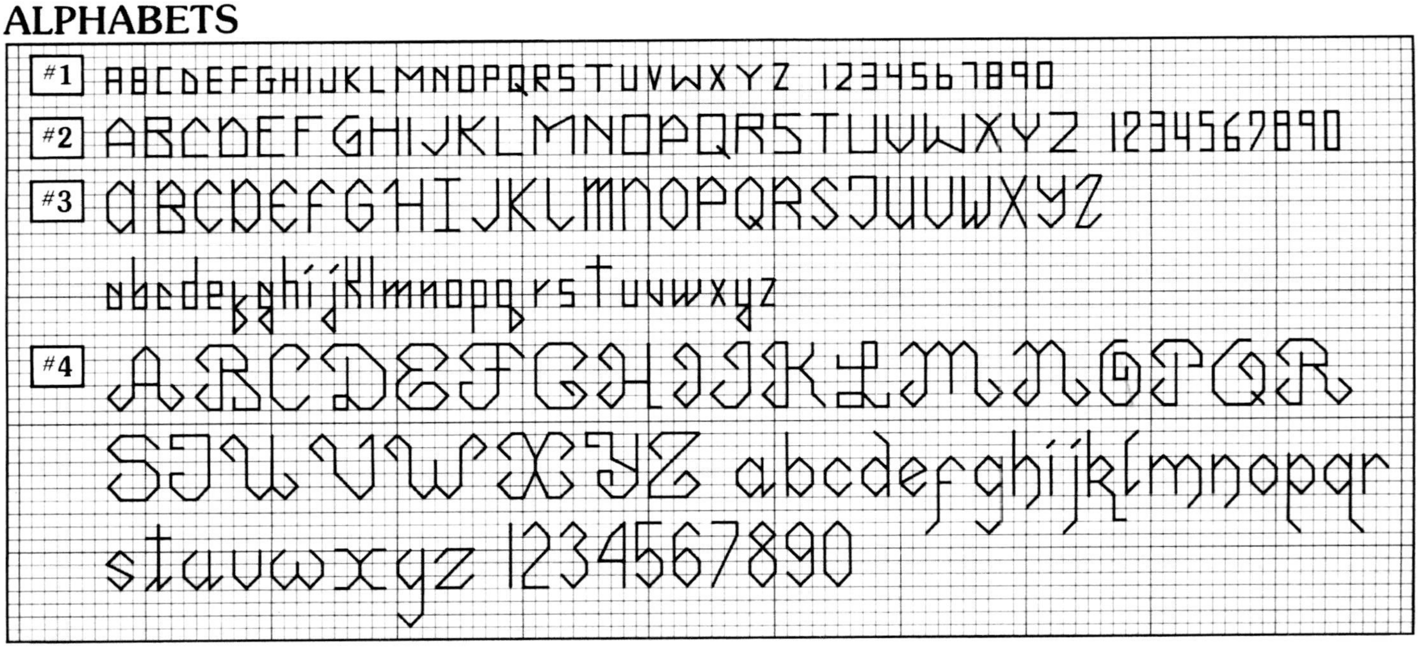

Made in U.S.A.